SHOULDER SEASON

Shoulder
Season

POEMS

Ange Mlinko

COFFEE HOUSE PRESS
MINNEAPOLIS
2010

Coffee House Press books are available to the trade through our primary distributor, Consortium Book Sales & Distribution, www.cbsd.com or (800) 283-3572. For personal orders, catalogs, or other information, write to: info@coffeehousepress.org.

Coffee House Press is a nonprofit literary publishing house. Support from private foundations, corporate giving programs, government programs, and generous individuals helps make the publication of our books possible. We gratefully acknowledge their support in detail in the back of this book.

To you and our many readers around the world,
we send our thanks for your continuing support.

LIBRARY OF CONGRESS CIP INFORMATION
Mlinko, Ange.
Shoulder season : poems / Ange Mlinko.
p. cm.
ISBN 978-1-56689-243-8 (alk. paper)
I. Title.
PS3563.L58S56 2010
811'.54—dc22
2009051508

PRINTED IN THE UNITED STATES
1 3 5 7 9 8 6 4 2
FIRST EDITION | FIRST PRINTING

ACKNOWLEDGMENTS
These poems have been published, sometimes in altered form, in the following journals:
    The Boston Review: Squill; *The Chicago Review:* Discretion; Schilderachtig; *The Colorado Review:* The Devil's Pollard; *Critical Quarterly:* Thalassotherapy; Shoulder Season; Corporate Abstraction; *Jubilat:* Tree in the Ear; *The London Review of Books:* Treatment ("We went to the vivarium . . ."), Stet Stet Stet; The Eros of Nothing; *The Modern Review:* Again, Again; Rocamadour; *The Nation:* The Children's Museum; *The New Yorker:* Treatment ("It's a little spa for the mind . . ."); *Poetry:* A Not Unruffled Surface; Securitization; Year Round; The Leaves Are Falling; Gaullimaufry; It Was a Bichon Frise's Life . . .; Eros of Heroines; Kouign Amman; Win-Win; This Is the Latest; *Web Conjunctions:* Camouflage; The Distance Between *The View from Nowhere* and *Put Me in the Zoo; With + Stand:* Trolling Dark; A Single Point of Failure in the System; *Zoland Annual:* Brooklyn English
    The author is grateful to these editors, as well as the poet Ryan Murphy, who published the chapbook *The Children's Museum* (Prefontaine Press, 2007), where some of these poems also appeared.
    In the poem "Discretion," some quotations are taken from George Santayana and Robert Cormier; the final anecdote was relayed to the author by a former professor, Michael Comenetz. The observation about good actors in "Schilderachtig" is borrowed from the critic Michael Wood.

For Daniel Bouchard & Beth Anderson,
friends and poets.

"Like that gather-
ing of one of each I
planned . . ."

—James Schuyler

TREATMENT

It's a little spa for the mind—seeing butterflies
set themselves down by the dozen like easels

on bromeliads, when out on the street the boutiques
are dilapidated, construction can't be told from ruin.

A single taste bud magnified resembles an orchid
but what that one's drinking from is a woman's eye

which must be brineless. I wonder what she consumes
that her tears taste like fructose. For minutes she's all its.

Then the moon rises and the river flows backwards.
Composed of millions of tiny north poles, iron's

punched out of the environment, hammered into railways.
Pubs serve shepherd's pies with marcelled mashed-potato crusts

and each tree casts its shade in the form of its summary leaf.
Is a woman's eye a single taste bud magnified?

Yet construction can't be told from ruin.
Out on the street the boutiques are dilapidated

by the dozen like easels. But the mind—it's a little spa.

TREATMENT

We went to the vivarium—to see
the tropical butterflies in a
walk-through biodome. They were
cocooning, their insides filled
with meconium. The chrysalises looked
like jade and rosy quartz pendants
for ladies' ears—with gold worked in,
something Babylonian.
Enormous specimens
breathed against tree bark.

Belated naturalists we.
I kept repeating to myself:
the mind is not a little spa.
The Mind is not a little Spa.
You can't retreat to its imaginary
standard distance
when outside construction
can't be told from ruin.
The butterflies set themselves
down like easels
on bromeliads, but their brushes
can't reach to scratch their
palette

CAMOUFLAGE

1.

Babyclothes made of camo—
There should be a Lysistrata in the forsythia.

2.

That blue one's a suitcase
fluttering midair:
satin within, camo without.
It's a security measure.

Just in case one hitches
to your jacket
you exit
by an antechamber,
examined,

sent on your way morpho-less

and carrying nothing over,
leave the airport

metaphorless.

FOR ALL THE WORLD

1.

He knew *bamboo*: "Pandas eat it."
We were sitting in the Chinese restaurant
admiring the living, jointed segments

screening out the winter in the window.
Someone mentioned it's a kind of grass.
The kind of family that reinforces

kindergarten's disjointed tidbits.
Pandas eat bamboo. Koalas eat eucalyptus.

2.

There was the lead bib and the prop between my teeth
in which film was slotted; almost instantaneously

it appeared on the LCD screen as an image of my jaw.
Incisors all the way down, looking for all the world

like phalanges, metatarsals: the x-ray of a forefoot.
When I returned, you were readying a folder of papers

beside a suitcase. Your contacts in Beirut.

3.

The nightly irrigation of the lawns at Akhawayn
sent scimitars through my clothes as I walked
from the library. They planted lilacs

for all the world as if those were dachas
there in the incongruous, peri–Saharan mountains.
They planted willows on the banks of man-made ponds.

For where there are servants—teachers—there must be swans.

ATGM

You're weary in the daytime, and at night
you radiate alertness. It's like your clock
has reset to a time zone in the future.
As in the poem, "There is a hornet

in this room . . ." someone else lies tight
with anxiety, though neither of you talk.
Lowered as if through an aperture
into dreams on a distant parapet

she's cocked at an angle, half upright
on the pillow. Earth looms like rock
outside the window threatening fissure
from a petaled 9M133 Kornet.

DIRT

1.

Zsigmund II & Zsigmund III in the Romi-Isetta.

Zsigmund II & Zsigmund III in the Romi-Isetta
up the switchbacks of Santos in the time of Quadros.

Up the switchbacks of Santos in the time of Quadros
they'll push the Romi-Isetta when it overheats.

Does this vision of Zsigmund II and Zsigmund III
driving to Santos in the Romi-Isetta

turn on missing him, in a jeep on hairpins
of the Middle Atlas, in the time of Hassan?

Or the hashish? or (but Lacerda was not an assassin)
reading—somewhere—that the CIA

taught the secret police to dissolve bodies in acid?
Romanov-acid. Not Romi-Isetta.

2.

Zsigmund and me on his Yamaha YZF-R6.

Zsigmund and me in an ill-fitting helmet
on a Yamaha YZF-R6 on Easter

a hundred miles per hour through Amish country.

His earliest memory is of a child-size panzer
authentic to the last detail, in Vienna.

At a hundred miles per hour on Easter
through Amish country, the orchards in bloom,

does this vision, at mortal speeds,
of a five-year-old boy in a miniature panzer

turn on a double-bind, and not Santos
or the Middle Atlas, or Amish country;

missed, then not missed, per the YZF-R6?

WORLD LIT

The crayfish in Tarafah's tank
in skeleton suit all elegance,
tail flexed daintily down and pincers limp,
looked at him askance.

Through the aquarium glass
all must've been magnified and blurry,
the wrong prescription to read
the helter-skelter textbooks by,

WORLD LIT the houseboat population
worried water to adumbrate,
narcissus on the lipped table
and for mascot, a ferret.

*

The surgical scissors Zuhayr finagled
(stoned on hash)
from the pharmacy supply store
with bold French
cut off the cast as Saturday night wafted up
from the cobblestones and trash
of Oberkampf.
Acquired it playing soccer;
that put Zuhayr off Venice.

But he split the sticky maple keys
and stuck them on his nose, sitting on steps,
speaking of mylar bunnies.

*

Near the broken campanile of the platz
an elusive cabaret
keeps an address.
Once, from the roof
of a madrasah Labid could see
across to Sale where an imam
under house arrest,
it was said, circulated cassettes
of his sermons for followers who marched
against relaxed divorce laws
on the frondy boulevards.
So when the cabaret door
(signless) emits
a green light from its transom
al-Harith blurts, "I think
if we cross that threshold
we'll be in Agadir
with the hated Germans who go topless
as the Kaiser Wilhelm Gedächtniskirche."

ENGINEERING

Lushness returns to Emmaus.
turning up the pilot
all set against
of the houses
double-hung sash window
in the landscape
Its sky-colored cooling towers
Callery pears
I feel the sensation of it
—just that one whitish curl—

A hyper-lilac
on dozens of Miss Kim blossoms
the Benjamin Franklin angles
with one candle per
There's more air
past Limerick
billowing over
coming into white
at the sight of the rootsilk
under hydroponic lettuce

*

Plein-air surgery
redecking suspended
filled with a millennium of silt,
and unfathomable
What a difference serifs make
Life Is Worth Living
in the Clearview font
(1) from thinking of skin
as if perpetually mid-kiss

the Tappan Zee's
over the 700-foot gorge
shad bone, and milt
tidal muscle
in the lettering of the sign
versus traffic directives
And it's a long way
drawn over cheekbones
(2) from being on *equal footing*

PEONAGE

A steel-stringed guitar emits its little riff.
Can I feel your fingertips? It's as if
the years reduce to heartbreak in Massachusetts.

Songs are torture massages.
Fingertips are shredded by steel strings.
Anonymity claims even these stirrings

heartbreak trademarked. Though dismal
the moral can't overcome the song's charisma,
and the self-inverting melody

can't contraindicate its brutal remedy.
Love will be organized like notes from a piano
emerging like ants from the furrows of a peony.

A NOT UNRUFFLED SURFACE

The sky was laced with Irish cream mist, that mellow tan
   overhanging the hills, which were studded with deathmasks
   and baskets spilling flowers from both ends.
We scanned the haze for lightning.
They were studded with earthworks and iron forks inserted
   between leaves of grass, jacks and bearings and balances,
   sinuous fingers of pink marble and synovial joints in bronze.
But if we got struck by lightning—not a lot; say glanced, or
   shaved, there is a chance (we heard) it wouldn't be so bad:
   a little refreshing, a little like *La Vita Nuova* in a readable
   translation.
"In a flash," as they say, we could acquire a self-renewing
   subscription to classical music (it's always classical in the
   scientific literature) accessible at all hours and piped into
   the forebrain from the hypothalamus.

This space available for celebrations.
Someone visits for the first time and says, "Oh, let's get
   married here" and guests drive in and eye the hors d'oeuvre
   tent before finding a folding chair.
But it isn't long before the mirroring going on between, for
   instance, the sculptures and the trees—the trees looking
   more like sculptures, the sculptures getting seasoned,
   growing bark (patinas) even—it isn't long before it
   hypnotizes the guests.
Who would wear a wedding dress in such a charged

13

atmosphere, having heard that ghost story of the wedding
dress with the power to possess the soul of the bride?

Actually it was a horror flick from somewhere, Tokyo or
Calcutta . . .

It was a wedding dress that took possession of the soul of its
bride the minute she saw it in the mirror, or it saw itself—
and this we know happens, but not with the malevolence of
this dress that wrecked havoc at the reception, set the hall
on fire, and dropped a crate of champagne on the string trio.

"Aha," cries the groom as he realizes the chrysalis of evil he must
divide from his bride: "You are hardly an unruffled surface!"

No, you would not want to wear that dress amid the wireless
network of gigantic sculptures and their wind-scraped
murmuring.

When the wind stirs, is it not the gardeners?

The gardeners are invisible, they don't garden during
business hours.

As you'd put a dye in the air in order to see it, a bird sucked
through its drafts advertises the invisible and upgrades it
to naked.

THALASSOTHERAPY

Envying binges
on unbandaged waves
"tumultuous come,"
I'm all "qu'est-ce que c'est?" when the jellyfish
ride out, the brainless meninges.
What remains of the rue.

Like the five-point harness
on child car seats
made of the same foam
as life jackets,
the starfish arches.
What remains of the crabgrass.

The life jackets made
of the same foam
as the bicycle helmet—
qu'est-ce que c'est—cracked in two
in your hands.
What remains of the butter-and-eggs.

The head unscathed
emerging from foam
as from a shell game
when a shell—qu'est-ce que c'est
—explodes.
Same foam as the bicycle helmet,
the car seat, the life jacket.
What remains of bog sage.

SECURITIZATION

In someone's distant algorithm
your mortgage was bundled to another's
—hedged—
and stamped a new "security."
While it was swapped
from investor to investor
accruing fees and interest at each turn,
your shadow
partner
defaulted
and she abandoned her home.

Someone uses your mortgage
to leverage
something
far inside the starbursts of a server.
Likewise marriage
has
no image—
What's a mortgage
and who's
it engage
on the other side of the firewall?

*

I witnessed a will
which—the language invested with law
godmothers the peacock's
fanned
screech—
would take care of the baby in the event of a
[blesses herself]

It lives at the cathedral
and seems to be some kind of
mascot for
baptisms

*

Securities:

The future art you'll make and its pleasure
is hedged against the
boys who died

you fancied.

WIN-WIN

If an orchidophage's tastebud magnified
resembles an orchid
So my buds indubitably mimic pricking ice cream cones.

Love, little by little it dawned on us the artisanal
ice cream, especially the prize-winning caramel,
would be out of our reach,
like the previous Friday of a Sunday leaving the beach,
in the meltdown.

When you gasp at the soundfile of cymbals
—"that knitting needle sound" through your headphones it kindles
an inkling that in the bongo-playing
you can hear the wedding ring,
ting ting in the liquescence.

When you hear the Sound you may smile
to think of the ones and zeros of that soundfile
resembling sticks and drumheads,
or knitting needles and drumheads
as the beat gets molten.

When things get molten you may think of a fire
made up of a million little matchfires
rendering a house on the Sound
—belonging to ex-employers—a bit of char on the ground
as the regrettable outcome of a meltdown.

A thousand hotheads make a Sarkozy:
at the sight of their BMW in a car-cozy
a thousand swans make a Sigolène
purring *win-win*.
The Sound is statistical, like the meltdown.

The holes in your socks and the follicles in your leg
are as pixelated as a JPEG.
My tastebuds resemble microscopic glasses of gin now, now's
the time to shake and shiver like a maraca in this house.
The many kinds of dissolution.

Well, birds happen forth from feeders like swinging pagodas
against snow, as
the meltdown goes on, a dump of rock salt.
We'll soon be signatories by default.
Crystals of sodium chloride

are made of smaller crystals of sodium chloride.
Let them know their house
is made up of many other people's houses, magnified.

YEAR ROUND

Two flags nuzzle each other in the desultory gust
because they are
fleeing the trees, who are cruel to one another, shading their
    neighbors to death

a mixed bag
advocating small business in a loose confederation:

the flags don't give any shade at all.

On the anniversary of our country
we throw dynamite at the air
we build into.

*

Daylight savings. A beeline
to a sea lion, as the children's song extols, or is it
a beeline to a scallion?

You hear your own accent—
or
a child makes an error to see if you're listening.

A heartfelt counterfeit.

*

A cough muffled
in its own sputum's
repeated
in the next throat:

a family of coughs comes
to couch in us
while the sun rises
over the church,
treetops' psych ops
combusting all over
the ground
tasked
with a snowdrop.

KOUIGN AMANN

I went to make kouign amann. It sounded Irish
and/or Maghrebi. But it's Breton, as I can swear
by the blue hydrangea like a cloudy iris

I photographed near Finistère.
And now I'm here in Croton-on-Hudson
trying to remember what was sinister

about the asymmetrical cruets,
swan and cygnet, I thought I heard
—listening under a sweet duvet—

duet. (But *do* swans vocalize?
Strengthening the pair-bond
while their two pasts together caramelize

the present?) Sinister like Croton's
name, derived either from a Kitchawanc chief
or Calabria, source of stonemasons

for the dam. The former translates as
"Big Wind," the second is known
as the birthplace of the school of Pythagoras.

Sinister not knowing if silent esoterics filter
down to our little dam, dreamt of under
sweet sweet down duvets. Bretagne's off-kilter

menhirs call to our bric-a-brac rock
like names orphaned after the glaciers' retreat
from Bricquebec to Wequetequock.

THE DEVIL'S POLLARD

Great angelic civic trees
cropped into Ys and Vs

to accommodate the powerlines appear
now that their leaves are sheared

as the wings (rather than horns)
of a dilemma, a diptych.

It's the realpolitik
of utilities—saying the powerlines

must be accommodated and therefore
either nonaction

is out of the question
or finding solutions to aesthetic injury

is too costly
(that the injury is more than aesthetic

and may weaken the tree is thought
a small but acceptable risk)

and therefore we have come to the tip
of one wing—

we'll argue no more: the other wing
is the bard naming

the devil's pollard.

GOURMANDIZING

Shaggy rectangular cows standing and lying on greening grass.
The all-but-abandoned stalls, the small silos, the margins of
    "farming," what we call "farming" exemplified by this
    Angus-filled paddock that belongs to a three-star
    restaurant specializing in locally grown organic food.
Here were the shaggy rectangular cows with their calves,
    in the onion grass growing gay tendrils, the onion grass:
    curling horns absent from the cows, which were gazing
    at us from their lounges as we passed on our hike, my
    babies cooing at their babies tagged like fur coats with
    anti-theft devices.

A storm dumped snow all day, packing the interglacial
    crevices of Westchester with ice, but our presences were
    requested that evening at the three-star, nay, three-
    supernovae restaurant by your imperial majesty, our Lady
    of Employment, for the *Christmas party*, a time to eat and
    be merry before the ax falls.
It was food for kings, robber barons.
Heavily Our Lady moved, along the tables, distributing the
    gift baskets.
Waiters, verily, specialists emceed the dishes that emerged
    with alacrity from the wings to perform their show.
The table a studio for simple sacrifices of, what, sumptuously
    appointed watercress, oyster and peekytoe, pommes de
    terre, Angus.

The storm dumped snow all day, the babysitter canceled,
  driving seemed foolhardy, I risked disfavor—
The Lady's Moue.
It was to be a ritual fattening in any case, and I missed it, my
  Last Meal, shut in with my babies while the snow raised
  the ground up to the faraway sun and now, as it's
  dropped back again, green, we're out for cost-free
  weekday entertainment, hiking, and come across the
  docile Anguses, built on rectangles (landscape, not
  portrait) arranged delectably around the paddock in
  families, with tufts of wild chive.

STET STET STET

Where the curve of the road rhymes with the reservoir's
and cleared of the leafy veils that for six months
obscured it,
the landscape's wet chestnut
in the gray descended cloud
intones You're lucky to live in a watershed
so no vast tracts of tacky drywall
turn the land into peremptory enclosures.
You've bought in.
The venial sin:
being exceptional.
Reading Hölderlin.
And the natural hallucinogen of joy
helium–cum–oxygen
leaving wordy outputs
hanging on piney tenterhooks
while all the wild protected liminal woods
contrive a blind.

THE EROS OF NOTHING

The icy clearances
where the trees used to cast their shade
in the form of their summary leaf
speak to me of
nothing, carried out to the letter.
Tempests, mountains—the grander genders
submit nothing to the letter.
The distance
between the winter equinox
and perihelion keeps growing.
But it will again be nothing.
The black under my nails reminds me
this day's mystery was in eating a pomegranate
with my small son and on my blue shirt now
—nothing!

Though when the blanched leaves shiver
silent chimes beyond the glass
brings either the rapture *[my children...]*
or self-criticism   of one who comes with a theory
[...are an economy of scarcity]
of myself there is no more evidence
to admit—only consistent
with limestone's incessant weeping
cave a madonna's
negative.

PENNY SQUASHER

An anamorphic octagon stretched across the wall
like a penny squashed in a penny-squashing machine

in some rest stop on the turnpike
catching your attention in some part of the brain

named, as in Everest or Antarctica,
after a Fissure, or a Ridge, or an Area.

As the sun crooks through, skewing the muntins and mullions
courtesy of a high ornamental window,

you remember the boys asleep, in car seat, in carrycot
whooshed through the nickelodeon lights

of the turnpike. Awaiting you was a glass
of cabernet like a magic lantern throwing across

some wall of the brain its anamorphic rubaiyat.
Boys asleep, unharmed, in car seat, in carrycot.

GALLIMAUFRY

Reaching for the vinegar over the range hood
(still dashing grass wisps on the gas flames
from the exhaust vent where we booted
      that brooding sparrow)

I remember the rabbit in the Tiergarten
that perched on its spatula feet where the grass
had just started to green. The German clouds
      were unibrow.

It's not the stretching, slightly weaving, that recalls it,
it's the tang of vinegar, Easter egg–dye solvent.
And my gallimaufry gets going, guests for dinner,
      the requisite foofaraw.

In the soffits of the staircase a rag and a feather duster.
In the eaves the nests made of frass and cellophane.
"When it rains on a golf course it's called Irish dew—"
      father-in-law's jackstraw.

"Dundee, is this an Aussie shiraz? Put it in the croc au vin."
Cellophane and frass. Everything in the canon
went into Gargantua before he was born from the ear beneath
      his mama's cornrows:

Augustine, Aquinas. Aristotle and Plato. Virgil and Homer.
Goliards and troubadours. Thus an ort peeking out
from a nostril, skin flakes, a slight acne, undercoat
      all colors, like a farrow;

the chuffer, snuffler, grunter, farter, pecker, whelp,
head half the size of the requisitioned teat
(Googling "mastitis" and finding "ewe," ew)
      —the whole shebang

reeks of bedstraw. On the radio, transrational statistics;
Brigitte Bardot lashing out at the leash law in Zurich;
on an uncle's fourth percussive sneeze the baby wakes
      —interrobang—

X'D THE GO-GO

"The liquor known as Lorraine Thistle has fallen into a discreet desuetude."
—ROGER-POL DROIT

You putter in the wooden shoes a lathe cut like gouda.
The tulips are redder than French for *blood* this year.

The rotten egg repellant worked against the deer
here shown (see the label)
taking a whiff and breaking out in plewds.

Redder than Spanish for *blood* are the tulips this year.

The black-and-yellow ruse in their if-you-please
is undeniably coaxing the nonexistent bees
nonexistently dancing over the stamens.
x-ing the go-go.

Bees' desuetude's in the news, headlines discreetly eking plewds.

TROLLING DARK

Is that an oak leaf or a hawk?

Actually it's Originalism
as practiced by the polka-playing,
weisswurst-boiling,
potato pancake-shredding
beeristas of Bear Mountain
Oktoberfest.

Maybe the ruins
are in the eye of the beholder?

For real; the ruins in the eye
that occlude a good view
of the moss-green lederhosen
and the tunic and hat
covered in pins and buttons
too small to read
from just the distance
that puts a man at three inches tall.

Meanwhile the oak leaf,
the hawk, the uneven ground
of moraine-stones
and squirrel-chew
come alive in the slightly
tinkling light,

which took a bruise
around the mountain
that deepens almost unto
the cranky troughs of
little Hessian Lake.

DISCRETION

"Furzy Jersey" isn't quite right.

A life of Hoboken after Hoboken . . .

"Your landscape is not here."

"I do not make a habit of losing landscapes."

I accept a cup of coffee on behalf of man's prejudice against himself—
"anything which is a product of his mind seems to him to be unreal
or comparatively insignificant" as the landscape draws an arm in
from the left but keeps its right arm flat on the horizon, or draws
both arms in, as rows of trees close up the view like hanging sleeves,
and the flatness is why Maryland is loathed until, rising on a bridge,
clothed—in cerulean tulle: the suspension like a row of legs
poised on the barre by a mirror and jutting from the jeté (à la antlers
from the startled buck in the x-ing sign) a metal comb. Fanciful!
And the shadows so sharp the tires hiccup over them like rumble strips
as if shadows gel, succumbing to the laws of physics.
There is some threshold, e.g. at which instances of "hither"
gel into usage. And speaking of tires, as full of air as "thither,"
there is a sign: "Millefueille Tires" right off the ramp.—Coffee helps.
"As close as Pennsylvania to Maryland; as far as Philadelphia
from Annapolis." It was while visiting, ever-so-briefly,
one of those townhouses set like jewel boxes in the jostling street,
as if Delft had never gone *pfft,* that I realized my abhorrence

of the housing development, for instance the one in Camezotz, PA,
where I spent some time as a kid riding a bike around a system
of cul-de-sacs like a video game ca. 1981, derived
from a prelapsarian innocence of systems; not to mention
nonstandard door frames, window sizes, variable-width siding,
and glass that à la its moniker, "slow liquid," attenuated
in some sense like a tear-shaped bass note, toward the bottom
of the pane.

          How to Wreak Revenge on a Town by Painting
Your House Orange . . . and studding it with white urinals (yes)
and the coup de grâce: a pickaninny butler with ashtray hand extended.
I have a hard time comprehending how people can feel such
ownership that they must prove it by defacement. The silence in a room
where you have recently spoken is different from any other silence,
and this is evident from the sound engineer who records dead air
for minutes on end after you have left. "We can take consonants
and vowels from all the words you've pronounced and make you say
things you've never said"; so the cushion of silence on which they
cut and paste must have the same consistency, must be the same silence
disgruntled by a helicopter. We can take consonants and vowels
from all the words you've pronounced and make you say things
you've never said. Here one rediscovers a prejudice for oneself.
And the idea that a room corresponds to a musical note
and thus "resonates" when sung to—the idea that even this bridge
might correspond to a B-flat that, when "sung" by the wind,
causes it to oscillate and utterly collapse—there are photographs—
suggests despite the belief that "we are satisfied only
when we fancy ourselves surrounded by objects and laws

independent of our nature," music is material, but "the material"
isn't *wholly* material. Speaking of which, construction materials
are *way* up this year thanks to the hurricane damage in the Gulf.
"You mean, like, the wholesale destruction of cities."
("I am not in the habit of losing landscapes.") When Ronnie asks
if your family is from "the other side" she has to use the phrase twice
before I understand "born in Ireland." No, born here. But "the other side"
conjures a mirror world doesn't it?—let alone the land of faeries, poetry,
and mirage that we normally associate with "Eire." I mean,
take the custom of posing riddles to strangers or choosing a question
which only one person answering to an identity could know.
The marriage bed hewn from a tree with its roots in the floor. Or
"What's your mother's maiden name?" On an island off the coast of Maine,
a summer visitor walked into a library and asked the librarian,
whom one imagines a woman of indeterminate middle- to old-age
grown into her role with its props, its pomp, its flashing bifocals:
"How many books can one take out at a time?"
"Discretion."

URUSHIOL

In the yellow-cake colored paperback in the basement
was the story of the woman double-dipped in gold paint
who died when men covered up the small of her back,
        the last breathing spot.

In the thick encyclopedias layering the shelves
was the story of the temple in Kyoto, where elves
(well, monks) painted urushiol lacquer over all gold leaf
        to preserve it from thieves.

But in a lost tale a daughter in the back seat
of a van with dozens of glittering, under a blanket,
bottles, lacquered, and boxes like jacquard, of liquor—
        gifts for customers,

or a heist?—is a mess of poison ivy under the blanket
with the spirits gilded and boxes elongate;
untouchable, though not dying. Spirited
        away like a scratching anti-Juliet.

SCHILDERACHTIG

Corot green

Wtewael yellow

Van Ruisdael brown

These and more smuggled out from art history
into a landscape just beginning
to smudge under the endless patting
of the pine branches whose dumbshow
deer amble amid
en route to picture books.

*

That the Flemish played "kolf"
on river ice with the sleek instruments
we recognize as clubs and not hockey's
crumb-sweeps;
that a man could be painted
in pince-nez in 1646;

43

we can note such facts but it is that
shadows follow their masters into water;
that the Seine estuary's ecstasy's met
by a sluice of lust.

The ecstasy reproduces
as laying paper on canvas
for a quick sketch captures its huckaback
weave.

*

The precision required to paint
a seastorm seems duplicitous;

almost as duplicitous as a good actor
who substitutes for technique the effect
of being two people at once:

the mask ajar on the actor
cool beneath an agitated surface.

*

The morning glory nautical blue
good as rope around the railings
where the grass co-opts the gravel lots
boats on multiple easels (they look
like easels) bare their hulls on, heretofore
secret under the waterline like a beret.

Anchors' swag of rust and bilge,
chains and cables adjacent the wet
paint hydrangeas; breeze blowing
on drying riprap. Fish coathooks
and an urn propped over the transom
of a coffeehouse at first glance an apron
cast in stainless steel; a medieval apron;
a suit of armor. A heart fibrillated
beneath it.

Not to have an ostrich stomach
swallowing all the junk nor to be
the Alfred de Lostalot of what's worthy.

*

Whatever the artist patents—Klein blue
or mocking dots—a daughter exposed
as the neck of a flower above a glass
of water: "Waterloo Bridge, Morning Fog.
Bequest of _____ in memory of her father
_____ and her mother _____." For paint
not to throw its own shadow
the brushstrokes cannot be at all like waves.
But why on earth does the water want
to be mountains?

To view descendants—
its brushstrokes change our borders.

EROS OF HEROINES

Sunset backlights some pine to . . . a caped sponge
and though I throw my gasp after a monarch there is no hitch,
no hitching either to its serape or the echoing orange
drawing a rope, horizon's double dutch.

    (MINA LOY + ARTHUR CRAVAN)

As blood hits the air & goes red, so I burst outside exhilarated.
He has thrown a tippet on the double-bass, which rests on its end-pin
the way a singer rests on a glittering stiletto
while the other foot slips on a banan—piano. The strings
are not the electrified wires of a prison camp, but she's the instrument
of his escape, leaving me to educate my feelings,
subtracting the red from night till a wine bottle dawns green.

    (LEONORA CARRINGTON + MAX ERNST)

I saw the chess players over their griddles, all the furor of thinking
swallowed like a song in a furred flute; so it must seem
when a small daughter disappears with a wife,
morning reabsorbed into a lambent priori.

    (JACQUELINE LAMBA + ANDRÉ BRETON)

IT WAS A BICHON FRISÉ'S LIFE . . .

Louisiana skies paddle north nodding hello to some exiles
displaced by floodwater, so we all putter in the bisque
in fretted dresses, alleviated by a fan. But we have nothing on

"Le Matin," in whose rococo frame a curtain sweeps to bare
a boudoir, a Bichon Frisé worrying something between paws,
begging the dulcet glance of the mistress whose push-up,

cupless corset, and up-drawn stocking border what they
fall short of, per the stern frame rippling like a cloud!
Even the candle angles to get a look in the mirror

engloving the scene. Why it is her slipper the bitch clutches!
The gentleman's reverie is elsewhere . . . Loitering
Louisiana stops to admire this engraving by "N. Lavreinee."

What a chevalier! It makes the smeariest sunset think
it's in a Restoration Comedy, in such humidity
chefs defer meringues. "Ksar Rouge," "Taos Adobe,"

"Gulf Shrimp"—a thousand names of soft-boiled
lipsticks fritter English as if it were French, meaning
meeting no resistance from the flesh.

THE DISTANCE BETWEEN *THE VIEW FROM NOWHERE* AND *PUT ME IN THE ZOO*

. . . The pinetum and what have you.
I cannot always be anxiously keeping my accounts.
With a sky bitten around the edges
to show us we're in Nature,
who's to say the book a two–year–old holds out to me,
Put Me in the Zoo, is,
of intellectual instruments, the kazoo
whereas *The View from Nowhere* is the cello,
low, low its voice, modest
as if buying stock in Lindt chocolates, for example,
were no worse a thing—
From that book on my nightstand
children march with their classmates in a double strand down
a main allee.
Tour groups curl thoughtfully around focal points.
The Japanese visitors have RSVP'd
the *genius loci*
by means of their couture.
But we don't have to reduce the mental to the physical.
We can have a dual-aspect theory
where I am not a private object,
and pseudocamellias are permitted their fractal of irony.
Next, ponderosas' upper reaches are blackened
as if a smoke painter traced a torch there
(and we do imagine this to be

an area of highbrow graffiti).
Because those pinecones are more like us
than we are like the 500-million-year-old
outcrop of gneiss and schist
around which we manicure narcissus
the parade of children seen
about twenty minutes ago
are now louche high schoolers swarming the café.

SHOULDER SEASON

On the strength of the light in the southeast
I could surmise this isn't the time for poinsettia.

Snowflakes hard as schoolyard jacks
fall from a cryogenic layer of air

eagles use as lorgnettes. It's unseasonable
judging by the light in the southeast.

The poinsettia has been delicately
loosening the bolts locking velvet bracts

in attitudes of warm jouissance
so that a cuticle of dried blood hue

encroaches on the edges of a lively red,
then altogether drops to the ledge a corpse.

On the strength of this I could prise
piccolo jonquils out of April edemas.

SQUILL

Half asleep, I heard a pin drop.
The quality of light was strong,
it was changing weekly, but on top
of every new change was a lung-
like cloud with a violet
or oysterish froth burnished to pearl
by an untucked ray. Sleep debt
would only let me half-unfurl
from what I could not be prised from.
At the far end of the hall, behind a door,
I heard a pin drop. In another room
on the unpolyurethaned wooden floor
where gaps were growing between slats—
I could distinguish the sound from
that of a screw. I knew it from a thumbtack.
What was that dream,
that brain candy cottoned to, the flight
from a battalion, a mane slipping my grip
—as my ear divined a button's bakelite
from a Lego—leaving page-worn fingertips,
the *vita nuova* every night rejuvenated
and dashed to bits by a baby's complaint,
my aural monitoring of his lonely play syncopated
with forays back into the dreamscape?
From its no-backstory,
to my daylit past in waking, to recordless

and unknown history,
back again to what I knew: the sound of a dangerous
small object falling from his pincer grip
to the floor. I knew it from a ballpoint pen.
A ballpoint pen from a felt-tip.
I knew the sound of his noggin
hitting the floor from the rattle
of a coffee mug. Jewel box, toolbox,
my ears' spindles chimed and tattled
out of dreamland, the dice in their cups
little movie screens on each side
playing different scenarios. A joke,
the child too quiet. What it belied
was that he might choke,
but I could hear what his digits dallied
and knew he was still gambling.
This is what it means to rally
for the future, as my father lambing
on all fours with him madly
termed "answering the call of life"
never knowing whence I came
or what dirt was made flesh on my behalf.
I grew the ears of a cat, tuft-flames.
I could have heard a seed growing.
A seed growing in their mirroring labyrinths.
Twin vegetal wombs in eustacian tubes sown
with squill, which when the moss is absinthe-
green in the brownscape, is alone
the smallest simplest flower in the cold.

First flower of the year, Easterish
and yet it could be a bold
spy device, an earpiece.
Its cells assembled from history
outside my own window, as the light
stepped up—threw down—in mystery.
And though you say it is right
that no one descended from Uralic
language speakers
has Uralic
language structures
pre-determining the cast of thought until
badly retrofitted in English,
I could not see this Siberian squill,
this earpiece, Easterish,
and not think of the cells of a language
in my sleep, growing out of the frost,
assembled from history, a burned bridge,
as the first division, from which I was lost.

THIS ONE AND THAT ONE

I.

She swears she saw, in this one's crib last night, that phosphorescence
that portends horns of a kind, fabulous appendages

when he proceeded to speak in ancestral gibberish.

II.

As a rhymer of "alligator" and "elevator," that one took satisfaction
in things that click.

It made his mother dream of switches on safetys simultaneously flipped.

III.

She swears she hears, in her own *mamanaise,* thoniers on a fishing-boat
haul in seine nets full of langoustines; cats enceinte in hyacinth;
tongues evolved to cleanse them of the telltale smell of meat,

the smell of meat on cubs, telltale bas-cuisine.

TREE IN THE EAR

We parked at 15th St. between 7th and 8th Aves.
After lunch on 7th Ave. and 14th St.
we walked as far as 5th St. then turned and walked down to 5th Ave.

Then turned again toward 7th Ave. at Garfield.
Walked past 8th Ave.
to Prospect Park West, veered
back toward the 3rd St. playground. Continued onward to 15th St.,

and stopped at the car. B. told me of his superior canal dehiscence.
He felt a fullness in the ears;
he could hear the vibrations of his own voice in his head;
his heartbeat;
and on bad days, the nystagmatic motion of his eyeballs as he read.

In Tullio's Phenomenon, the sound of music instigates vertigo.
Rilke: . . . *da schufst du ihnen Tempel im Gehör.*
I felt for him, even as I sensed
he was turning into the hero of an allegory
in which even to sympathize (like strings)
was to add to the vibrations which were his torment.
Fenestration is an obsolete surgery.
. . . und machte sich ein Bett in meinem Ohr.

We stopped at the flea market
where old books caught my eye:
a Russian primer, a Portuguese primer,
and a German primer.
I already had a few words
of Russian and Portuguese under my belt
(obsolete: baldric), strange as the combination was,
which owed itself
to particular historic circumstances—
a grandchild of DPs—
and wondered if the third term comprised a sort of cipher.

Interrupting my reverie was B.,
who noticed a copy of *Invisible Cities*
which he claimed was not only his favorite book,
but one that he had
superstitiously not finished,
so he could continue to look forward to it
indefinitely.

If there were a word for this,
it would be a German word.
Like the leafy promenade
that divided the belle époque mansions
from Olmstead's park: boulevard.
Where I had strolled with my son
for the first three years of his life,
but which he no longer remembered,
for that cherub no longer existed.
O hoher Baum in Ohr!

The Conservatory
is just a fieldstone house built early last century.
We could hear the strains
of children at their lessons
through heavy doors.
Standing in the crosscurrents
of melodies emanating from unseen lodgings,
we wavered.
"Ear training" followed,
as the music teacher strummed
a little meadow for gamboling,
strummed a little strand of trees,
strummed a hoofbeat of deer
then taking out a glockenspiel
glissando'd a little stream,
glissando'd a bit of pixie dust.
"Spin. Pedal. Skip. Turn," she commanded
through bars of melody
measuring response times,
gauging the ability
to *attend*.
Glockenspiel, but also
other exotic words: harpsichord,
harmonium, lute,
dwelling now beyond the general orbit
of the ear, here shyly coaxed back
to greet the children,
as fauna emerging from a boscage
into this ephemeral glade.

SYCORAX

Your eye is too bark-brown to tell
if your pupil has turned rectangular.
Yet you leap as if a goat's bell
egged you on, around the annular

path in this preserved forest.
We are where the wild things are—
Wildflower Island's closed to the tourist
of its funguses and feldspar

but rambling on the vestibule, alert
to danger where the pines resemble racks
you call what's underfoot "chocolate dirt"
and if we can live without what Sycorax

knew—the lore of plants—their terse
glamour leaves me abashed:
poison ones can curse without knowing how to curse.
Perfect circles where alien lichen splashed

prove them adept geometers.
And ferns flame where their spores crashed.

THIS IS THE LATEST

Lobster in the bathtub Christmas Eve
Scrub the tub first Hand off cleanser
Rinse well We don't want Comet
in our lobster He's clicking
against the porcelain Everyone leery
of going to the bathroom
Bubbles had risen when we lowered him in
now he's limp Stare into the water
that wears a similar gooseflesh
The lobster is dispatched

Wrapping an oversized box (a coffee maker)
can't find a swathe of paper
big enough Start to cobble bits together
with tape (ah— chitinous)
and the joints begin to look like
repeated segments of a carapace.
A pilot blue glows Haemocyanin—
a blood based in copper not iron
while the broth of something Provençal
sings from the pot a little tomatoey

a little stigma (not stamen) of *Crocus sativus*
under the Star of Bethlehem

If the universe is
bouncing
and shrinkage
pendulum
an infant's sobbing
have a prosody
it has the chemistry
or our bouillabaisse,
a primal soup contain
and nonspeech

in the briny speech stream

—this is the latest—
between inflation
as if on a trillion-year
why wouldn't
on the exhale
as on the inhale
of tears and seas
indeed,
—besides babbling
and raspberries—

a scuttling underwriter?

THE LEAVES ARE FALLING

Here I am saying "The leaves are falling"
—one of those choruses
that vie with interminable verses
to mock hoarders.
Yeah, we get
that a palette of winds
is a pretty thing:
one blurs the anther, another
the river splurging on riprap,
expunging
phosphates,
out of the temperature
differential building
sculptural fogs
that promenade
between shores a glacier
wedged ajar, a fjord.
Whatever gives the river
its seriousness reverses
in the light
of those clouds moving
as if absorbing
their pomp in advance of it—
characters
which untied the painter
and took the sculls again.

MILLENNIUM OPTICS

(For Alicia)

This bracelet wards off the Evil Eye,
A. says, smiling.
She slips me the envelope from Greece—under, of course,

Corinthian filigree, willy-nilly, the hotel's decorative moldings.

*

Amid the communicating hallways and escalators, rooms accessible
through other rooms,

sudden applause through nautilus walls—

I only touch the mirror rim once, when I think I am lost
between the glabrous sky and a pigeon's glare.

*

A planetarium squats on the peninsula.

I could walk there within the hour
and put my eye to the keyhole at the angle

of the funicular at Gibraltar.

*

Love's game is hide and seek.
An Orlando would make this city Arden.
But the glass disappears us like surveillance tapes

continually overwritten.

A SINGLE POINT OF FAILURE
IN THE SYSTEM

The peninsula of *The Peninsula*
is topped by a swimming pool in a crystal enclave,
its swimmer protectively eyed by idlers
in mounted conference rooms.
Some conference rooms are called fishbowls,
some offices are glass boxes abutting nil
on one side, hallways on the other.
A muting weft introduced to a harp
becomes a carpet swallowing steps.
Cordy is the "single point of failure"
in a system that generates 160 million
thanks to his proprietary algorithms.
Cordy wants twenty thousand from the budget
to build a mirror site near Rutgers
thirty miles from the "blast zone"
among the pick-your-own blueberry farms.
It has no windows, three security clearances,
with three concrete shells protecting the servers.
Ah, Cordy. A change in orientation, a swoon
may find you walking toward the tip of *The Peninsula*
which meets the ladder rippling from the moon
and calls laundry service to press small wake.

Interlude: Cordy's Dream

Every town has its partisans—
here the neoclassical detail on a facade,
side street, is an unmessianic frippery.
The airy expanse is like putting on glasses
so the almost alpen gallops disclose they are hills.
No, flanks. No, hills.
Even the neon signs read vertically.
Butt ends of carrots, wine bottles,
plugs of cored peppers litter.
Collecting the bill envelopes, inserts,
wrappers, third class mail and circulars—
Someone's taking the recycling out with frozen hands
when the difficult wind chooses then
to explode its data all over the streets of Peekskill.

Three men proofread in a dark room.
Once Rabelais, Carrot, and Percival O.K. it
the doc's ready to be embossed.
The basement presses are trembling:
Everything smells of materials.
Plate Embossing Devices
emboss each braille dot onto zinc plates, oily,
malleable, raw-edged though—careful!
A second check from Percival,
Carrot, and Rabelais is required to ensure
the plates are ready for the presses.
After being used to create many copies of paper braille,
the zinc plates are recycled.
However, if there are three errors
the Library of Congress rejects the book.
If three books are rejected,
the Library of Congress contract is voided.
If Percival is the single point of failure
Carrot and Rabelais are terminated too.

Interlude: Percival's Dream

Oil derricks in Azerbaijan
are reflected in their incontinent puddles.
The tankers like blood balloons in the harbor
travel hazardously
across the sea, under glaucous sky like dappled zinc.

My scarf folds and loops abstracting its pattern,
blindfolding the caryatid in my throat.
Yes the caryatid in my throat
holding up my pediment, pentimento
of Indian summer on fall on summer
peeling back a russet on a green, a Russell terrier.
November dandelion a chandelier
where I sit on the phone taking notes
from a man who wants the last line to be
"I guess we'll have to live in the lighthouse."
Yes "We hate the city, we hate the country,
I guess we'll have to live in the lighthouse."
I cock my fountain pen, adjust my scarf.
Ghostwriting Personals for clients
whose happiness depends on Love
and who have, possibly, this late in life
only words left to romance with
makes words carry the weight
I always daydreamed they would:
desirous words men in a dark room
would caress with their fingertips;
irresistible words men who coaxed
money from money would gamble on.

Interlude: My Dream

The autumn leaves smell like whiskey,
bitters, and vermouth, that is, Manhattan.
Let's live in the lighthouse
erected where the peninsula lies down,
and from an enclave overlooking freest swimmers
I'll continue to work, spellbinding books.

CORPORATE ABSTRACTION

In the weeks after the catastrophe
I reported to work only to brood at my cubicle
and feel the trembling of the river
like a Rubicon.

From a yellow window
in a Class-C building I couldn't tell
a battered slip of paper in a downdraft
from a gull.

Downwind, the Battery.
Coming up the west side from the park
I felt the trembling of two rivers
the moment they fork.

To walk to the smoking pit on my lunch hour
to see through the fence
and stand there on tiptoe
to match the suspense

of the iconic sculpture on the square
which the rube
in me thought stupid, balanced on its
corner. *Red Cube.*

AGAIN, AGAIN

I had watched the bumblebees working the bullseye
of the sunflower, whose hairy neck could no longer bear

the weight of the frazzled head after a storm.
I brought the sunflower indoors to die slowly sipping

through its ragged straw the tap water I'd infused
with a tincture of the household staple "Mirabilus Grossus."

Just as a lowly Joan Quigley set the date
for Reagan and Gorbachev to meet, mightn't the star-chart

that sets the sunflower season's perimeter,
coinciding with that of certain storms rotating up

from the Carribean, equally predict the fate
of a meeting between a fleshy artichoke and a tureen?

Just as a lowly psychic might guess (turning eyes
of a sunglass rack) a toddler's likely to declare,

"Again, again!" so the star-charts could tell you
toward what point on the horizon the sunflower fields

near Volubilis would turn their faces on a day in August,
when the lemons would trickle back to the *marchés*.

Walking by the Christian bookstore noting books backs
turned toward me in the window.

Out there's a moral law. Within I've only stars!

ROCAMADOUR

It's an El Niño Christmas. But then, it always is.

O because one is never *là-bas* for long,
holding an infant is like going to Paris.

. . . And there I was, in the Latin Quarter,
cathedrals propped like viola de gambas.
"Tariq, do you hear the peacock?"

Muleteers' dates fall for them in a comedy.

We are looking for a mnemonic, already
the infant is outgrowing his hammock.

Already new knowledge is obsolesced.
Student housing: a tome held open over the head.
Gray limeade of rain on the quays.

And then the flight to some mystical flowering Algarve.

Holding an infant in a somnambulist's daze.
Angel wings accents, acute and grave.

BROOKLYN ENGLISH

The liftoff from a rooftop coop
distant thunder of the icemaker
child in a tenement stairwell
a cement echo in the art deco
shambles: these are not the
terms to discern a sentence by,
except a sentence that wraps
its back in a negative embrace
against you, made a fence.
It is a sentence so philosophical
naturally asymptotic butterflies
shudder to land on obvious
subjects, topiaries.
(Monarch migration season—
a Lincoln-slept-here glamour
to the rose-of-sharon.)
Perennials flare out of lots
in which legs of chairs
suspended in the tangle extrude
hidden toys in the foliage
and last blossoms like teacup sets
smashed till only odd ones left.
When tractor trailers roar past
tripping anti-theft alarms
we all cease to speak, honoring
the uncertain fate awaiting things

whose words retain the sound
of verse: victoria, brougham, caleche. . . .
The sky has an ardor for clouds,
avatars of lambs when lambs
populated the vocabulary.
Take the treated flannel cloth
that in jewel blue'll rub the smears
out of the lenses, put on glasses.
Spiderwebs on underside buttresses.
But now, reader, get ready for
a *real* scene of horror:
There's not a word demanded of you
by all this air and leafery. Not a word.

THE CHILDREN'S MUSEUM

1.

It's hard to know whether today or yesterday was the full moon;
excitement isn't rigorous. It's just river–silvering

blent with the odor of silt where the roofs spike
along a repurposed waterfront.

A beach ball floats above the pressurized stream;
it is disequilibrium that keeps it there. Soap's expressed

as blisters when even gravity works backwards
at the limit of the ball held upside down inside the loop.

Rewards in a game they play against themselves
—"Fancy *curtseying* as you're falling through the air"—

the shade breaks up beneath the oaks
tithing their gifts against the curriculum

of an armed galaxy. It slides into focus for the instant
I'm brrr, blurred.

2.

Rocks grown sagacious wigs along embankments
and then verandas rounded to embroidered iron,

boarded windows, clothing drops. The dive bell
lacks eels out its portholes, but "double-hulled"

nests two U's as it sounds. Nearby, a first draft
of the helicopter, patterned on a Chinese children's toy.

("I make you a present of everything I've said as yet.")
The ice wigs' molecules vibrate, but in a gas state

they're distracted, and at their most congenial, this:
—at the thickness of its muscle I recoil—the river cuffs

full of self-healing tears or self-buttoning froth
(like the governor vaned with goosefeathers)

stranding me among inventions,
with myself decked. Even mirrors are painted on.

COLOPHON

In honor of our author's Hungarian heritage, this book has been set in Ehrhardt type, which was designed by Miklós (Nicholas) Kis. After taking religious orders, Kis traveled to Amsterdam in the late seventeenth century to learn the arts of printing, type design, punch cutting, and type casting. He not only learned these skills, he excelled, creating an amazing number of outstanding fonts during an estimated ten-year period. Then, as planned, he brought his new skills back to Hungary and printed several editions of the Bible and other religious books in the Hungarian language before his death in 1702 at the age of fifty-two. Perhaps it was because he was a humble, religious man, perhaps it was because he was a foreigner and was no longer around to claim credit, but whatever the reason, all of the fonts he created in Holland were initially attributed to other designers, including Janson and an extensive range of Greek and Hebrew fonts, in addition to Ehrhardt. Only within the second half of the twentieth century has the full range of his achievement been revealed by typographic historians. The full impact of his work on the development of Hungarian publishing and culture is still being evaluated. At Coffee House Press we lift our mug to salute the many unknown artists who contribute to our shared culture.

FUNDER ACKNOWLEDGMENTS

Publication of this book was made possible, in part, as a result of a grant from the National Endowment for the Arts, a federal agency, because a great nation deserves great art. Coffee House Press receives major operating support from the Bush Foundation, the McKnight Foundation, from Target, and from the Minnesota State Arts Board, through an appropriation from the Minnesota State Legislature and from the National Endowment for the Arts. Coffee House also receives support from: three anonymous donors; Abraham Associates; the Elmer L. and Eleanor J. Andersen Foundation; Allan Appel; Around Town Literary Media Guides; Bill Berkson; the James L. and Nancy J. Bildner Foundation; the Patrick and Aimee Butler Family Foundation; the Buuck Family Foundation; Dorsey & Whitney, LLP; Fredrikson & Byron, P.A.; Jennifer Haugh; Anselm Hollo and Jane Dalrymple-Hollo; Jeffrey Hom; Stephen and Isabel Keating; Robert and Margaret Kinney; the Kenneth Koch Literary Estate; Allan & Cinda Kornblum; the Lenfestey Family Foundation; Ethan J. Litman; Mary McDermid; Rebecca Rand; Debby Reynolds; Schwegman, Lundberg, Woessner, P.A.; Charles Steffey and Suzannah Martin; John Sjoberg; Jeffrey Sugerman; Stu Wilson and Mel Barker; the Archie D. & Bertha H. Walker Foundation; the Woessner Freeman Family Foundation in memory of David Hilton; and many other generous individual donors.

This activity is made possible in part by a grant from the Minnesota State Arts Board, through an appropriation by the Minnesota State Legislature and a grant from the National Endowment for the Arts.

NATIONAL ENDOWMENT FOR THE ARTS

MINNESOTA STATE ARTS BOARD

TARGET.

To you and our many readers across the country, we send our thanks for your continuing support.

Good books are brewing at www.coffeehousepress.org